Dedication

This book is dedicated to a rebirth of a part of the lost gospels that had to come back into this generation to help stop confusion and conflict between the people.

Could these words of endearment come from a disciple in the past to a present day messenger.

This book was edited by the author and staff of Bound to Heaven Publishing/Ministries.

There have been none who approved this book before its release.

Foreword

The Lord's Reign

The real level of rights that people have been denied is one thing. It is spiritual rights. The lack of them has caused the division of people throughout the world. It is the real thief of all times that has turned more people against than self and all of the wars of nations against each other.

Then all of them put together and the in-house fighting between one color of people against another color. That is what the lack of spiritual rights that has been misplaced or missing in the presence of the lives of people has done.

Therefore, we reclaim the right to have spiritual rights delivered once again to the land and the people who will appreciate it on all levels of showing it as we live among one another no matter what color.

There have been missions that have been put together for the blessings of the people for their hearts to see the light of God.

Public Notice

To help people so they can understand themselves is all I can do my best at doing.

The Plague

That is in Michigan was caused by the people with towerism. Stop the people with towerism and stop the man-made plagues.

To not think too highly of myself gives me strength to keep moving on.

Become not conformed to this world be transform to study war no more.

There are a few paragraphs within the last chapters that were needed in this book to fulfill the understanding of an upcoming book titled *All Peoples Handbook*, that gives the wisdom to become blessed with the ability to receive spiritual skills and what they can be used to achieve to become a blessing to others.

How much money can also be saved by using the book *The Disconnection of Extremism*, to help eliminate the radicalization of people. How much can be used on other things the USA needs to have done also that can be saved to aid to the understanding of this, book *The Recovery of the U.S. Government*, to clean up within the American government first that help others not want to dirty up or harm America.

Now to prevent the past from repeating itself. We are in need of a lot more wisdom that we can live by in our lives.

Clump is being derailed by another Bush off of the trail, to end his run for the position of president. I am doing this to help put an end to this thing called towerism and the spiritual warfare in America.

To learn of the way to give or get a clumpectomy, go to Amazon.com, search Bro. Tracy Bush. The eBook is ready. Start with Cleveland, Ohio to Help safeguard America.

The Beginning

Hello to all we are seeking out the help from people in many ways. Get this message out because there is a new level of thinking in America we fill the people are in need of knowing about.

We the staff have put our minds and hearts into this, we are sending you this memo to inform you of an upcoming event. Please past the information along to as many people you can tweet it out. This is what's happening.

My concern is I am not a Republican at this time but I would at least like to see a fair fight without Satan weighing in with his spirit that could create harm. Now this is how we all can try to make thing right.

Therefore I submit this information for your review to use your judgment to reveal the truth to yourself then join in to help prevent what could be one of the biggest mistakes the American people could ever make since the country has been established, I hope we share the same judgment.

There has been a new spiritual development of wisdom presented to me. It is directing me to a position in making the world safer and better place, even though I have never extended myself in the area of politics, I found myself compelled to write about the injustices that have been happening within the ranks and the propaganda of the unethical level of things that are not right, done by the some politicians along with the prevention of what could be done, if the American people are not aware of who they are voting for and what their capabilities are that can harm the public at large.

The redevelopment of a new level of growth

A candidate has mystified a large number of people in America. The people need to become expelled and released from this trance which a clumpectomy can get it. Get fed up and you will really do something about it.

This book is like self-administered, self-healing surgery to release the seed of denial out of one's self or the truth.

People get your crazy in control and don't get with someone else's crazy. It isn't healthy for you.

What Do You Think?

To help the world: if we the small people don't try to untie the knot the country is in nobody else can; stop spiritual warfare.

To The Nation of People

We present the fact of what makes the people lose faith in the leaders on a layman terminology to recreate the order that came from the Lord and not mankind.

David against Goliath

Sometimes you got to make b.s. that others want to see to be used to get their attention out of reality in order to bring reality into light; the actors that are better than best with the miscues not too far gone.

Prevention

For the people in the Republican Party from having warfare that hasn't yet become full-fledged within their own ranks.

On Our Own

We can do something to help keep humanity safe without the finance, as a people to stop two problems? 1. The in-fighting about the voting process for president and 2. Keeping our land safe from terrorist attacks.

Zone Out

One of the number one things people need to divide up is time with themselves. It is a tool that a lot of people do not use enough. For some that don't it causes them to have issues because they don't think out the right action. Then they pay a price that causes too much on one level or another. This is what could be a partner to Satan and we don't need any of his tricks to trip us up along our pathway in life.

A Note to the Wise

Now in these days do we really have to take sides all of the time? Why can't we learn to go with the flow to what we know are the right things to do? Think about it.

Now can both parties accept that right amount of wrong has gone on long enough to bring out the truth in congress and both parties change some of their ways?

An unhealthy way to get caught up in, where some got hurt clumpatizes; feelings can be restarted to help move the people forward, that can cause harm because it puts people in the void-noid to move themselves at a time when trouble is moving their way to a degree they may get caught up in it. This is what can be fixed before it gets broken or fix it if it is broken before something bad happens.

It will be better to take a bruising and keep on cruising
Than to not take a Clumpectomy

If you are a republican and don't want to allow the front-runner of the party to be a duck you are guaranteeing to not let him win with this methodology. With him as a leader, that is what it will be like for the country, we will be sitting ducks right alongside him!

At This Time My Mind Is Running Like A Jumbotron
So All Can Know This

If we were a republican and didn't want a tower in the White House maybe you should choose a democratic president. Therefore, if we pray for the right leader in the White House that is what we will get. Promoting these causes can help save an important part of the White House. This is to help elect the best candidate possible not the lesser of two evils.

This Can Work to

Take Down Towers

If we start from the top and work our way down to fix a number of problems in the USA.

A Miracle That is Real

I can use this scenario if someone is stuck on someone else's "ism" it can be called, let's say clumpism, which causes clumpitis requiring them to have a clumpectomy to cure them and save them from themselves.

From today and this day forward, can we say welcome back to the heartland of America.

Who has the most party members with towerism?

This could be the biggest mistake American people could ever make voting for Clump. Don't blame me read this book. Every voter who wants to vote for the duck needs to read this book first before they vote. The reason I am emphasizing this point is it is creating a level of spiritual warfare in this country that we have to avoid at all costs no matter how you feel about a duck because the country will suffer.

Are We the Ones?

I have to lead the charge to help save the country from going into rough waters. I have been chosen. I didn't volunteer.

If you really love the country before you cast your vote, you need to get the 411.

Get the 411 before it is another kind of 911 that can be prevented. It will cause a spiritual turmoil between people and open us up for another kind of possible air raid.

It is the spirit of the Lord in me that is leading the charge and/or the spirit man

How Can This Be or is it a Calling to Be Fulfilled?

Now could this be one man's quest to right the wrongs of the country like a David against a Goliath? Does one man give a way to all to be a part of stopping the duck from getting to the White House by claiming no victory for him?

The Redevelopment of a New Level of Growth

How Can This be Done?

With the information within a book titled, *Fixing What is Broken in America By Stopping Towerism*. A problem whose time has come to address, that will aid big in the recovery of the U.S.A., in all private sectors of business levels and the government. This book helps assure that the people who live and vote get the best civil servant they can in the elected office to serve within the governing body, by this wisdom helping to give the elected official a way to right the wrongs within themselves, if needed, to do the right things and change the pathway they are on in order to do a better job, and show a love that is unconditional to all the people they serve. Now if the people are truly tired and fed up with the way this county has been going and running by big business and the government, this may be one of its greatest ways to have a chance for the people to make change.

If you have a need to know what we can do to fix the problems that the USA have, starting with the fact we need to help cure some people who are afflicted with clumpitis by helping them get a clumpectomy. The sickness of clumpitis was born out of towerism
Has this candidate mystified a large number of people in America? The people need to become expelled and released from this trance which a clumpectomy can get it. If you are fed up then do something about it.

1. Are you ready to put the country back together again to make it greater than before with no tricks involved? The latest information is at your fingertips. Fixing America will require the wisdom people need. The book is mentioned above.

2. What got the republicans in their mess? With the current party leader, it is their towerism. They could not see the forest for the trees, so they let the duck in.

3. To learn of the way to give or get a clumpectomy, go to Amazon.com, search Bro. Tracy Bush. The eBook is ready. Help safeguard America.

4. Do people have the element called clumpitis who thinks he will get the job done? If so, they need a clumpectomy. The perception for this is in the book about fixing what is broken in America.

5. It calls for a clumpectomy for those clumpees who have clumpitis. Now what does the duck have? Towerism.

Again, I will remind you, this is about heading off and stopping the spiritual warfare trying to start in this country.

Beware

There have been so many other countries and nations that have fallen prey to this kind of problem in their land and without fixing it, it has caused irreparable damage to all levels of living standards. To prevent it harming us in the USA any more than it has already, we must wise up and stop it.

Thinking of the future, the use of the possibility of being able to detach a person with bad intentions that want to harm others can not only be used to alert the right authority at a time of great gathering, but after the upcoming major event, but during day to day living. How handy it can become.

Now the process of development may not work for everyone, I am sure but if it is acquired by one in a 1,000 people it will be a blessing we all can be thankful for that can help to keep us as humans a more content and happy people.

Perception

We need help to continue the mission that we are on at Bound to Heaven Publishing/Ministries, we need your prayers. The ministry is in a stalemate or gridlock that needs to be broken, one way or another, by people buying books at Amazon.com, search Bro. Tracy Bush or place an order via the website, www.boundtoheaven.org, to see the selection of other spiritually based books of all kinds. For example, to remain a blessing to the people who are in need, to keep up the promotional work we are doing and to help in the cause of not letting the wrong kind of towers of power in the government and other places they can cause harm to people whether on a short term or long term basis.

Dump the Clump
See and Know

Voting power of the people of our country has taken on a new face that it has never known before. Therefore, it may be somewhat a spiritual war that we can win with the Lord.

With this information we can also help stop any inside distortion that a naive person who may be in denial has about their shortcomings.

Republicans

You have an internal spiritual level of warfare that you are going through that has toppled over a process in the system that you are used to as was in the past whether you won or loss, except for in the year 1952.

Now how can you put things right in your own home party? It is only one way accepting the truth. Like it or not or face the self-destruction that may occur due to the uncompromising level of not accepting the truth.

Though freedom is a click away that can be spread like a wild fire or like rain to douse the placement of a person with the process of a thing called towerism in or out of the way to prevent a set-back, your party may not make a come-back from in a 100 year process.

Democrats

Using your power to let someone cause their own demise is where the business at hand should be because they may have handed you a victory and it is yours for the taking due to the fact that they have been caught with their heads in the clouds and could not see an enemy of their own kind that crept up on them and unleveled their own playing field to a degree it created a kind of quick sand that if you just tell the truth with what you learn about towerism you will continue to see them sink their hopes to take a victory in the White House, believe this truth and receive the victory to claim the spoils that no greed can have because you created the miracle of blessings to be shared. Need more information, email tb.bthpm@gmail.com.

If you really want to know what a brother's keeper is doing. It is what I do.

What I Have Done Lately

A Peace Offering for the Police and for the People

Distributed press releases all over the USA; gave books away free on Amazon.com and in printed format; had a kiosk billboard located just outside the justice center in Cleveland Ohio for 6 weeks. All promotional expenses have been out of pocket. Featured in interview on 710AM radio in New York City.

Why Do Black Men Harm Each Other More Than Others?

Stopping black on black harm: promoted positive information in the community; voiced aspects of my ministry in open air formats, including but not limited to various local radio station outlets; issues involving police and people; attended various rallies; gave away free copies of books online at Amazon.com; visited local businesses and organizations promoting and selling the book; did a live radio show with the police.

Disconnection of Extremism

To help stop the recruitment of radicalism/extremism/terrorism; ran a campaign for a free give away of book on Amazon.com.

The Unwounding of the U.S. Service Men and Women

Service men and women in America are largest committers of suicide; gave away free books both in print and online at Amazon.com. We need to start a process to help decrease the number of military suicides.

Fixing What is Broken in America By Stopping Towerism

Ran a campaign for days leading up to primary elections in Ohio and five other states, during that time books for free online at Amazon.com; passed out flyers all over the city of Cleveland; sent emails/tweets, etc. attaching flyer throughout country to various media outlets as well as democratic and republican election headquarters. The voting of not the one with towerism – stop towerism – the outcome helps stop the problems in many ways people are having in life!

Read and judge for yourself to be able to help head off a possible national dilemma.

A ghostly presence of a spirit in America came about because of hatred and bigotry that took place in the 50's and 60's. We witnessed this as black people who were being subjected to brutality. White people showed outward hate toward other nationalities also. Now it is displayed in a different kind of war zone that has shown up on a spiritual level more so than the physical one as in the past but now it is somewhat reflected to all people that have the opposite opinion. That is today's dilemma that we all can repair by working together as one with one spirit.

Mankind saw and knew what he was doing before but he cannot see nor does he know what he is doing now. One was physical the other is internally spiritual. To add a combination of understanding, what we are developing is preventive measures for stopping spiritual warfare of and within the people of America. We have developed three books (*Fixing What is Broken in America...*, *The Disconnection of Extremism*, *The Recovery of U.S. Government...*). This fourth book is developed in conjunction with the other three to stop spiritual warfare in America. Assistance to all of these books can be accomplished with the help you will be able to receive from the All Peoples Handbook to enhance your spiritual skills

The facts are clear that if anyone has become radicalized fighting for a faction that is committed to killing others even the innocent, they have already lost in the battle of self with spiritual warfare.

Towerism is just like powerism in oneself somewhat at one in the same.

To fix it, start at the top and work to the bottom it is a not bottom to top thing as usual by knowing you can get down safely because what goes up can come down.

If you are cooped up with towerism here is a way down and out today before your walls come tumbling down on you or someone else and the walls don't only be the ones outside of you but the ones inside of you could hurt as much or more, depending on how much hell it carries with it someone has to repent from over or about.

Is the Lord's warning us with this book? Do the people sense and fear this unknowingly and that is why they are acting out? I think so, in and with raising hell.

I'm not saying this in a bad way, but if you think our commander in chief didn't do a good job and you let someone in that has towerism you are in for a rude awakening and you don't have to take my word for it but I pray it never comes to pass or to our future America.

Now if the person got into office we the people would have to be on our toes 100 times more than we are now to watch people to defend ourselves and that still may not help us prevent an ungodly act of aggression to us as people in America.

We the people have to fix ourselves before we can fix America the spirit of the people is so out of tune it needs help first.

I Had to Admit

I am a messenger and a shepherd also. I am the principal caretaker and shaper as an author with the many books we serve the people with.

To Understand the Depth of this Scroll

You must know that it has come from a place that put it in order in the upper room where saints and angels come together with the Holy Spirit to put in order strategically ways to help make things better for us humans, also to prevent things from happening. It is as simple as that.

Before anyone can experience this kind of offering they will have a level of requirement that has a power of a kind of anointing that money can't buy or a person's wisdom can't pay for. In saying this, I implore you to lend me your ear to hear about this measure of caution.

As Americans, we have been forewarned about the state of our political system and as some of you have been given insight as we have been given the presence of the Holy Spirit to write about it.

There is a placement of redirecting the outcome of this upcoming election that needs to take place and if it is not carried out, I feel it may be one of the worse outcomes of a civil process the country has ever known.

The plans are as follows: present the individual who is now leading the Republican Party that could be the new president, to a new level of a peacemaker with the people in a way that gives them some hope and not like he has presented himself as the fighting kind of man. How do we do this and why do we do this?

1. We do it with love details example if the duck loves America then why would he insight fighting
2. This is done to show a way to understand his true self as a person with towerism
3. The plan then unfolds to show people the way to know who and what their candidate is all about. Then watch the truth set them free.

Until this happens people will stay blinded by his persona. It is not just that they are unseeing and unknowing, but they are afraid of what is happening in the country but also in the world. What needs to happen about that is it needs to be removed and the one big fact that no one acts like it is not there right before our eyes. It is a spiritual war going on and it has begun to rise up to a physical war that is now taking place in some people.

It is just the beginning of a way that people have to be rescued from if not it opens the door to the outsiders that want to come in and make it worse than it may have been in a way in this country since the civil war and we are not yet over that, believe it or not.

Therefore, I implore you to take and put on your halo about this issue or take it off in the presence of the Lord in a way that you may need to. Let your comment reflect your desire to help increase the body of Christ.

Now the plans are laid out in print we at BTHPM need your support and prayers to prevent a bigger problem than this country and world may be ready for. I claim the victory in the name of Jesus. The charge is on my heart and yours and I do need your help.

Footnote – you may not get the president that you want, but you won't get the one no one may end up wanting.

Know when fear becomes stronger in you it is like another being that fight to stay alive. But when you know this, you can defeat it with the peacefulness you have developed.

Learning that ignorance dies in people that sometimes causes pain but when it passes it is the way some would say as the silk worm has to die to become a moth to die to live.

Know when you come to the end of one journey of knowing fear, without fear you are at the beginning of a greater you in finding the values of yourself.

People are Submitting to the Spirit of Evil

If we have been warned who will not take the blame to the grave, to know that if you are in need of food and the lord tried to feed you and you turn him down it is as bad is when people were hungry and you did not feed them.

The pound of prevention can prevent a state of mayhem that may befall the country.

Make It Happen

To Help Stop the Outsider of the Body of Christ from Perishing

We are in a position to strengthen ourselves from not allowing the recruitment of people in factions that want to do harm to people like ISIS and others. But what about the one recruiter of the soldier that does this; is that not doing harm to himself as well? Do we have the right tools out there to stop this from happening that is on the outside of the church? If not, we are still fighting a somewhat losing battle, until we get our defense on the front line to stop the war with some people who don't know what they are about to go to war with themselves and wind up on the losing end of it, who don't make it to a house of God or know anything about what is really going on in their life.

That is where we need to be in our walk to get the people in touch with themselves. It is the bigger help we can be out in the world and that don't include the house of God until we get them there!

What Can We the People Say Can be Capital Gain for the Writing I Do?

It is to create a peacemaking alliance to show people how to not look at the fact of imperfection as a way to enhance them, but only leads to a dysfunctional way that makes them become more dysfunctional with actions of an execution that doesn't give them the wisdom and insight that they can use. This keeps them in a kind of gray area that comes with the territory of life at times.

The capital gain I am speaking about can make them fulfilled in a daily walk and talk to share with others without reservation to keep a pathway clear of the dark side of evil doing and thinking that tries to penetrate the mindset of some who are somewhat left in the dark in society or life's mainstream of existence.

This work may be known as the gathering of the flocks that are outside of the flock of people who lock them out because of one reason or another. To fulfill a wish of the presence of God where no man can go, not even me because it is the will of the father that he has presented to his people that Satan wishes to have. Satan has become a handicap in a way from the body of Christ by others on an unconscious level that the church of man doesn't want to see into the kingdom of heaven, believe it or not.

They put on blinders to not see a section of people and then take them off when they enter the doors of the house of God as if they are in a ritual state of mind without giving a single thought about it. Therefore, the commission of this writing has been done to enter into an unseen and unheard covenant with the part of mankind that has been affected by mankind's so-called prestigious and pompous attitudes. The word of the Lord has to come at this stage of grass roots to cover all his people because some things can't be taught to some people just in the house and it is somewhat better learned outside of the home before entering. Now comes the fellowship with self and the Lord.

The books give a way for people to be able to stop the vision that Satan has for them, to break down strongholds to individual's lives. A fear of an unknown process that places a pack of lions in front of the steps you want to take can be removed and the bondage of being captured in a dimension of being lost in a harmful reality can become the thing of the past.

To know you are loved by the father and feel the love he has for you daily in your mind, heart and soul to free the spirit man in you to learn to soar above the clouds of darkness that make you think it can keep raining on you have no more jurisdiction over your life. This makes up the whole process of learning and then some.

There is a way maker in you that you may need to meet and begin the process of healing on whatever level it needs to be held in your life, without the razzle dazzle and all the hoopla and winky-dink stuff that some folks may make you think you need to go through to be delivered from a place of darkness that your life is waiting for to be blessed from in order to make yourself right for the flight when time comes.

What is one of the best parts of going through the process of growing into the Lord's arms as a member of the body of Christ in the shadows of doubt and fear? It gives you his personal friendship and fellowship. You learn to adapt to others and when you go into a church service, your spiritual fellowship is needed to bring down the Holy Spirit's presence in the congregation in even more of a mighty way than others.

You didn't develop it from a click or a trick or a ritual that some have learned to do. It is somewhat of a manmade process of praise and worship, even though it has adapted to the state of religious practice. It may have condemnation of a not so genuine presence of a spiritual experience. Therefore, don't let the counterfeit cause you to separate yourself from the Lord.

The book in combination also gives the building of the one process that everyone can depend on about the Lord, if you put forth a little faith in him and try to keep going and growing with it. No matter what you may have done that didn't become a part of his liking, he will allow you to grow your wings of hope that lifts your faith even higher upwards toward heaven, within his presence into the light that creates goodness that will show on your outward being of who you are and what you do.

Free yourself from what could be the worst part of your life which makes you feel uncomfortable in your own skin, to a level where you are going backward in life. You need to take a walk on a God given side of getting to really know who the Lord is and not just thinking you know who he is. People who do that only confirm that Satan has a stock in them and an investment on their soul that they can't see or believe it even exist.

This is because you are helping to keep yourself blind to the truth. You believe you know the truth and think you have some insight that only you need to keep you in good standing with the Lord. It is only because of his grace and mercy that you are even able to see the light of day until you place a stench foul smell in his nostrils and he doesn't want to smell your presence on his earth anymore.

So be aware of what is ugly that may prevent you from seeing another day break while on earth. You can only be warned so many times before your time comes to an end or runs out of whatever way you want to escape, whether you like it or not.

Therefore, don't think you are okay and okay doesn't exist in heaven. The earthly life you share or possess is not the same as the heavenly life you wish for. You will not see it because you won't get there and know that no one is to blame but you.

What Does Man's Real Presence Mean?

He is to endlessly advance himself. But if he doesn't know where his presence starts or ends, it is because he is lost out of himself. That is why we learn to get out of the lost column of life to the found to use the wisdom of the Lord so the endless way can become as clear as one of the most beautiful days you will ever know within your heart.

The gift of freedom that is shared has been taught to me in the spirit world by a person who was once a man with a title of a priest that led me through my darkness to a light. This allowed me to write to others to help lead them away from the spiritual warfare that they don't know how to fight. Everyone doesn't learn to fight with the principals of darkness and only the Lord can do this for people.

Therefore, the dividers and conquerors must be learned and you must know whose fighting is to be done or you will not know when to back down at the right time. You will lose a way to a victory that wasn't yours in the first place. This can bestow the wisdom to know the difference if you are willing to learn; from a man with a great love for humanity.

Now maybe you can be at peace with who I can be with you in the presence of my writing as an emissary, envoy or go-between that can help you see out of darkness and create light within the house of love. Additionally, to let people know the way out, in order to recreate them so that the Lord welcomes them into his nest of peaceful blessings.

The goal is to help move people past others' "isms" they can get stuck on, with the right logic that pulls them to reasoning without seeing the fine print. Now one of the points I am making is, this state, if it keeps going will lead the country back to a somewhat state of Colonialism.

Being stuck on someone else's "ism" is not healthy. It could lead you down a dark pathway where when you awaken from it as others have, you find yourself at a loss for something in your life, whether it is tangible or intangible.

This is why you need to work your way out of your own "isms" first and know that one day all of the powerful incorrect messages in this life that people have, will become powerless and this will pass before all mankind at the grave site.

The power of the "isms" will become only known to the world as it was. It is not a crime to anyone but one's self to not see the division that creates smoke screens that blinds one's self especially if it is of a person's own doing.

That is why to lean on someone else's understanding to a degree where it blinds you and you no longer want to see the truth outside of the truth in one's self on the level of I don't know why I feel like I need to put the blinders on, is somewhat ludicrous.

Therefore, don't work with one of the prince of darkness' levels of presence. That is ludicrous and it could be a close kin to Lucifer. Don't let yourself be led down a primrose path of an illusion of some kind of grandeur that has thorns that tear apart some others who are innocent and harmless to you for the fame of it all. Nothing more or less because you can't accept you have been blindsided by a fool or a friend in thinking they are equipped to run a ship they don't know a damn thing about.

Get real with yourself and stop trying to fool others because you are somewhat foolish. Now, peace out!

Now let's get our dream in the right state so it won't fall on us. We want to believe in living in a better land but that isn't exactly going to happen right now. This is because we must become better people first. That is why things are the way they are. We are gaining some ground but if we don't become better people we will never get to the so-called promised-land that we wish for, no matter what we do as a people or who we elect as a president. Just because the world is looking at him, and he can say things to make people feel good, that doesn't mean it is not a smokescreen once he is in office and chaos begins. Let this fade out and not vote for the emotion of a talker who can't be a doer.

Lose the people who need to stick a foot up their own ass and pull it out again, before they try to put their foot up yours and think you need to pull it out and that is why they did it. Who am I talking about? Mr. "Think He Highness," or Ms. "Think She Highness," both are "Think They Highnesses, with a high tower kind of style.

Am I the wiser to want you to learn of it spiritually or am I the unwiser to try to get you to face it when you may not be capable of learning it? The answer can be learned and can only be told by the hands of time.

The crazy part of my life was when I was a warrior in the taking down of the towerism in a person who turned into a terror and murderer. His name was Hightower.

The no. 1 goal is to break their state of existence as a clan of people with towerism by informing them about something in the personal persona they have no idea exists. They might have an indication that something is wrong with them as a group of people who want help. It is unfortunate that a person has been singled out but it is necessary to bring light to this problem in order to end it. I hope you understand.

My aim is to help gain the upper hand on a handle that Satan has been using on people for only God knows how long even though I give a more clear explanation in the book that is helping to stop towerism in the USA.

My aim is also to break the system down to help pull some people out of that atmosphere to start to stop it from existing and to prepare the future generations of politicians to not get caught up in the way of living, because the world has had and been too much of a part of the secret of Satan ruling us in the darkness, while it is still light.

Therefore, if you have the right insight let's take this opportunity to make the most of it and at the same time we can add the extra help that may be needed in our cities to prevent a possible act of terror or horror that someone or a group may feel the opportunity to take advantage of to come in and do harm to people and destroy a part of our beautiful cities. That may add up to lives lost and pain to family and friends, as well as millions of dollars.

This is one chance we don't need to take if we can put another measure of additional protection in the lives of people we love. Some of the people in the towers don't want to even look out for their own selves and others like them and want to say it doesn't exist - the idea of a kind of secret society of people who don't exactly know about themselves.

I need not say more but if there is an ounce of truth to what I am writing about, we may be in for a rude awakening. If we do not try to break apart a collective body of people that will be in our midst and the storm they could create that may have a kind of fallout that reaches out to bring harm to the people of the cities in our land. My prayers are that it doesn't and at the same time we may have this opportunity to break the grid-lock on a political system like this in the lifetimes of the world, to change a process of democracy that has needed to be changed for a very long time. In God's name we can work together.

Acknowledging this Fact

Now right when America is about to go under, we get a spiritual and moral awakening. At the time I heard someone say this, I was working on this process.

What Two Can Easily Do, Don't You Know?

How do people get paid to help protect the city? With free reading material to help free people of spiritual warfare; we can pay ourselves by preventing destruction in our country caused by spiritual warfare.

A State of Alert

They are calling for the people to become vigilant and help to protect our cities and the people, but what do they give them to work with, any kind of tools? No, not a damn thing! Therefore if they want to get help, they should give help.

How can they do this and with what tools can they use to do this? First of all, it does not need to be manmade, in this case. It must come from a higher power. This must be something totally new and practical and compact that is not cumbersome and can be carried around without any detection to be less obvious and not be seen.

What could this be other than a gift from a higher power that gives insight that is out of sight to others until it is revealed to someone that can help to save the lives of people and some kind of harm or pain? Knowing what the power of the presence of the Lord can do to prevent a problem from happening is a way of life that most people can't understand in a sense to a level when it may come down to being forewarned of something before it happens all of the time and some of the people that may have this kind of gift and power of a spiritual anointing may not even know they have it. It can be us, by the people in a general way in life in a pleasant way that gives insight to a could be injustice before it is done, through a vision. So why not use it, or at least give it a chance.

Therefore, what is wrong with trying a new way of a kind of development of love that the Lord may want us to have and use. It was working for me and I am a somewhat ordinary guy who has had my life turn upside down at one time or another. If the Lord can work with me, I feel he can work with anyone who is willing to let him.

This is a part of my story. I think this is a great plan for defense and the good part about it is it keeps on giving a way to show love after the voting process is over.

As an example, when I was young, there was a rapist/murderer in my neighborhood. I was afraid for my mother's safety. The identity of that person was revealed to me in a dream. I was then able to help expose the person's identity so they could be punished. An old lady in the woods when I was very young told my parents that I would be special – need I say more?

If you haven't heard me by now you may be in a void-noid level of disbelief. Therefore I say take care of yourself. Besides, the convincing way of thinking is towerism that protects its own, but in the case of the denial they didn't and are they getting ready to even miss the opportunity to see a better way to fix something wrong in our land and the way we have treated others. That is even worse than what is happening to them now as a party of people who can help them prevent another kind of displacement of a part of life that no one needs to be lost in conflict in if it could be prevented, because of the blindness of a people who are supposed to be looking out for them.

The writing is not on the wall, the writing is in the sky that has no ties with a spirit of darkness but it is a part of the real lighthouse in the kingdom. Let's say they walk away as future losers of the presidential race. What could be there greatest asset they get to take with them? It is to understand what may have had them over a barrel in a way that got them stuck up on the inside of themselves and not knowing how to unstick themselves even though sometimes they wanted to. Also, how to land on their feet if they were one who didn't know how to get themselves down out of a tower that they created for themselves or someone else put them in or they inherited.

Therefore, they are bigger winners than ever and the people of the country benefit also. But the reflection on the world of how fast we fix our defects and to see us in a new light – how blessed everyone will be!

How do we impact the nation? It is with the love of the Lord that can shine through us all. Now you know what I am talking about and I have started so please help me catch up with myself and the work I do for the Lord; or, stay out of his way because his will, will be done on earth; like it or not!

To Clear Things Up; What are the Benefits

1. Prevent mayhem and rioting;
2. Give people hope that they are safe in our cities;
3. Show the world that our nation has loving atmosphere; and
4. It all develops a new level of growth within our country and for its people.

Now here comes the biggest blessing of all. We get a chance to show the Lord that we can be obedient to what we need to do and learn for ourselves – that is priceless and no one can put a price on it! All of this and what will come out of it I can't determine because only the Lord knows. To go back over the way the government may be run from now on after the placement of the healing blast of a state of freedom that could create a new growth and cooperation. Then a new level of confidence the people of the country will have.

Now as far as the democrats, we have the same kind of plan but a twist on it to give them a level of freedom. Because it affects their party only in a different way but towerism does exist also. Now could this be the best thing to happen to the USA that will not only bring this country back to a better than good level of growth? I don't know but it is well worth the try to see a brighter day and the setting up of lighthouse in the government on all levels.

Now, I say Amen and Hallelujah because of the best part of all this is it creates a place of peace where the Lord doesn't let confusion in. Getting from the messenger's mouth – there is not a hotter ticket in this country to be had.

The Lord will tell you if you have the job, how to rearrange the process of thinking in the right terms to truly make it easier on the people as they work together for the people in the country. Believe and receive the blessing of discernment to know what is right to do because mankind can't know it all and he doesn't have to pretend he does in cases of life or death, in whether people are treated right or wrong, whether people starve or not, and foremost, whether it is the right war to fight or not.

Getting in the wings of a higher power is a life quest that we all should have or at least desire and strive for. This information is enough to choke a mule. But you can get your throat clear.

What makes me think that I am qualified enough to present a level of insight such as this and help change the course of this country and possibly a major part of humanity? It is not of my power or my will that I succeed in doing little more than what is required of me to just present the information and facts.

If you are looking for any kind of track record that offers a courtesy of knowledge I can only supply you with the work that I have been doing throughout my years writing and developing my publishing ministry. We can go as far back as 30 or 40 years, when I stepped out on faith in believing the purpose for me to give insight in ways that are continuing to develop; to step it up to the latest phases of work that I have been commissioned to do.

A Plan of Peace to Win
No Matter Whose Side You Are On

It is time to put the halo on for a peace plan together because this isn't a fight of the earthly kind. We are in a fight of a spiritual kind and if we don't let the Lord lead us to victory we can have more casualties than we could ever imagine because Satan will sneak in the back way and do his thing and whatever it is it will not be good for the American people.

Now it is up to you to work with the plan that the Lord has given us or not, I am only one person. As I said before no violence or anger can win this fight. It is an order of peace that can win with the presence of the Lord in the midst of the people.

The reaction of fear is not to be in the presence of the people. It is the truth that will bring freedom and order to the disorder that the prince of darkness wants us as soldiers of the Lord to display and we have to be committed to not falling into the trap that Satan has been setting us up for, for years.

The time has come for us to take a stand together in the country as one in this moment of time to not allow the real enemy to harm us. We can defeat the presence of dark days sin-drome from the harm it wants to do to the American people, without being fooled into a fight that all people will lose out on something one way or another.

Therefore, here is the plan that the Lord has sent to us to use.

This is a book to end and win the spiritual warfare that was caused by someone with towerism. Now what a way to introduce yourself to politics and to bring about a war of this kind and not know exactly what or why or when it was brought into the existence of a campaign that you were leading a charge on, in the first place.

How preposterous is that? Satan uses anyone that gives him the opportunity to present itself to come up and out of its hiding place that some are not aware of, that has been instilled in them until the right time.

Now we can truly understand the process of what it is about; towerism, and we all are witnesses to the workings and goings on within the process of how it can use a good and or not so good person because it doesn't discriminate against anyone and it loves to show up and show out. When it has someone hooked, it did it to power and tower them up where they don't know how to get down from their perch because the daylight up there on their perch has blinded them from what is real and that is the problem they can and may be causing.

Now what a crazy way to take a stand even though they should know better and in the case if it is money they are after, they may already have more than their share but it is not exactly about money, it is a power that is fueled by Satan with the personal madness to conquer something at all cost to others.

It is like a person with a Dr. Jekyll and Mr. Hyde sin-
drome to defeat themselves at a cost that they
subconsciously want others to pay for and at an
expense that has no limit to it as long as they can
generate the adrenalin in themselves or the
endorphins that keep them high off the product of a
kind of self-incarceration. It fools them to believe it is
some kind of love of self that they believe they can't
live without, so they keep it up. How sad and mad it
makes the people with it become when it hits them.

The good part about this is only one thing. They wake
up before they hit the grave. After that it is better for a
rich man to walk through the eye of a needle or it
before they die they fess up to the truth about
themselves.

The Lord has heard the cries of the people and has
given them an answer to what they need to hear and
know. Now will the people take heed to the will of the
Lord?

This is a Warning

Within spiritual warfare, the fight is not won by
whoever is weak or strong, but by the righteousness
of the truth. Now you must be a bystander and not try
to stop or get in the way of this fight. You and I are to
become bystanders and see how the working of the
Lord takes place to defeat the enemy of his people.

If we as a people get between the Lord and the
enemy, more people will get hurt, as some have done
in other countries; when a spiritual warfare broke out

and the people became angry and fought on an earthly level and state of mind.

Therefore take heed to these words and what they are telling us we must do to know the power of the Lord and how he works for his children to protect them, if we let him. It is not about the enemy feeling your presence all of the time. It is about waiting to see them defeat themselves at times in lots of cases, for most people when they start or get into a warfare the Lord steps in to fix. How does a man know when he is ungodly? Well not all do until they die.

We can remove the dark clouds from above to let the sun shine through to keep the followers growing strong.

Find a Place

Whoever is a part of a party who is stuck on obstruction and filibusters because you are stuck on towerism needs to find the right space in their heart.

There are family members of colonialism; dictatorism which is next to terror; terrorism; threatening; harassing; intimidation that create an overall somewhat degree of hate that mesmerize people as if it puts them under a hypnotic spell of an unnatural kind that may make people feel weak, vulnerable and somewhat powerless against the defensiveness to that kind of person once you get somewhat caught in a cult-like atmosphere and then if a wolf pack mentality pulls someone in, it can be like a powder keg that may explode. We need to free ourselves from this bondage.

Now to defuse it will require the truth to take off the wick in order to defuse the harm. It also requires the wisdom to know what caused it in the first place and that is what is shown to the people in words.

What may have been the problem with the discovery of this problem in the first place is no one wanted to dig a hole and pull a snake out of it for fear they would get bitten because I believe I wasn't the first to know this kind of illusion of presence of the kind of people who straddle the fence and really want to stop. It is time to set up shop to make Satan hop right out of our pathway of progress in our political and governmental system.

Some call it foresight in a matter of urgency of a matter of importance. I will say it is the preparation of the Lord that is in place as it has always been when people listen to what he is warning us about, if it has something to do with mankind, that has been changed by Satan to perform a duty of graveness to harm his people.

In the word of the Lord there have been many wonderful things to become aware of and the fact still remains that some things are so unconventional that we as humans have a hard time distinguishing them, such as the man that the Lord said he would build his church on earth on his faith in a way it helps people to understand not being his exact wording but the meaning is the same. The name was Peter and even Peter said what he said to the Lord. Here is the scripture: Mark 14:29-31 29. Peter said to Him, "Even if all are made to stumble, yet I will not be."30. Jesus said to him, "Assuredly, I say to you that today, even this night, before the rooster crows twice, you will deny Me three times."31. But he spoke more vehemently, "If I have to die with You, I will not deny You!" and they all said likewise.

Then in verses 70-72 of that same chapter we get to see the nature of a true believer at its worst, when pressured by the outside world. 70. But he denied it again. And a little later those who stood by said to Peter again, "Surely you are one of them; for you are a Galilean, and your speech shows it." 71. Then he began to curse and swear, "I do not know this Man of whom you speak!" 72. A second time the rooster crowed. Then Peter called to mind the word that Jesus had said to him, "Before the rooster crows twice, you will deny me three times." And when he thought about it, he wept.

Now the point I am making is the way to understanding this is and can be at times only found by faith that can't be seen, but it can be the substance to come if you let it or if you stop it if it is a warning from the Lord.

Therefore, instead of looking at things as a war zone to happen in our country, or anywhere else, let's look at it as a greater way of using wisdom that has been planted in the people, that now can spring up with the new concept of win, lose or draw. We will fight the power that be, if Satan is the motivating factor behind it and that is who we see and not a man but a mankind victim that he is using as he always has.

The time has come to know we are able to stop this kind of manmade curse that we become a part of, but by only using the power of the will of the Lord that resides in all of mankind; in the name of Jesus, the beginning of a new era for the love of God in and from us.

As far as I there is no I in me because of what I can do since no man can write out a prophecy unless the Lord's hand is upon his hand in order for him to understand what is taking place in a part of the beginning, the center and the future of life, and even if he denies that fact of what the Lord said, he would say it is only a human trait to fail at times but it doesn't mean quit. Do you see what I see now or will you ever see it in your lifetime?

What may be one of our biggest problems as humans now? We always want a quick fix on our lives or things that have something to do with our lives.

Now, if we want to truly have this done over this matter we can ask the Lord sincerely to remove the enemy within the present state of our being who wants to use us in his spiritual warfare that is done in darkness that he wants to bring to light in our being. You can say "Lord remove the enemy from my life on a mental, physical and/or spiritual way that it has entered into my soul and especially in or out of my heart." Now say this and believe this and the Lord will do this.

The empires that some people think are good are just smoke screens for the people with towerism. If you are one with it, now you can get out or down without pain.

To stop him from advancing anymore in our lifetime making it better than before and take down strongholds of Satan.

This may sound far off the beaten path but there is an inkling of truth that comes with it look at the saving grace it can bring to light.

One of the main books I am working on completing that can make people able to see the possibility of someone that may know or not that has harmful thoughts or upcoming actions, is titled _All Peoples Handbook_, that enhances spiritual skills which is a gift that can reveal and ward off danger and let people know who it might be that wants to commit the act with violence.

This may occur in a dream or a vision that someone has that can be shared with the authorities to stop and or apprehend a culprit. It all may sound kind of far out there, but if it works on any level, even if it scares off a person who has the idea of doing something wrong. It is truly worth the effort to put it out and make this information freebies available to the public.

Let this be the will of the Lord that will give them second thought of if they do anything on the level of just thinking of an action the wrong way. It could be stopped by the detection the Lord reveals for someone. It was revealed in a dream, it was done in my life.

All people need to set up a new grade level of the way we produce love for others. If we had an overall grade could it be raised to a "a" or "b" because it seems as if it is a "d" or "f". How can we do that? First thing we can do is remove the dollar signs that we have in front of us that determine how much love you have for others. That's right a lot of people do this more than

41

we may even know. So if you are without lots of finances, learn to love others anyway and see how much further you get in life.

As I will remind some of you, if you are setting aims on a higher than average level it may require more of you than you are really ready to give that leaves you out of some of the main principals of life. One is the deterioration of the love you have for others that can hurt you later. So you must determine this for yourself. It can blind you and make you dysfunctional. The desire and acquisition of wealth can affect people living true to themselves. Others automatically get affected by them and that is a fact. How can it be changed? By simply stopping the ways of pursuing too much wealth or becoming overly wealthy; this works, try it and see.

If this hasn't been enough to put you in a steeple to be able to ring the bell that calls to present a new time and day with the fellowship you may need to read and start studying the Holy Bible.

In Conclusion

As a new cluster of stars has been found you and I could have paved the way to a process of helping us as humans grow into a newer level of peace and love for each other on earth. I say if we learn more when we are facing a plague that is created by Satan through us as humans and succeed, we can learn to repair and fix even more things that are broken on the planet.

Therefore, let's stop wasting time and keep striving to better ourselves thanks to loving the creation of the Lord.

Voyeurism Can Stop

An Unknown Trip of an Undetermined Kind

1. Stopping a spiritual warfare that can open us up to more of the work Satan wants to do to hurt people and it is not about America, it is about he/it gets in where it can.

2. Exposing towerists to start ending it. Find a new sickness even if it is a spiritual kind and fix it.

3. Make the people know of this to read between the lines themselves in closing.

4. Start to heal the country of bad politics. This can also help save a part of the world.

Are you one of those individuals who was born into, sold into, volunteered for, tricked into, or just had no other direction you felt, that is now within the lost tribes of the earth's process of little or no growth?

Excerpts From All Peoples Handbook

This land we live in could never become a land of milk and honey as some preach, unless we stop following the pathway of the ungodly.

Do we understand what the presence of having eyes in the back of heads really stands for or means? If not, it is the extra sensory perception or the combination of the extended special conduit that can receive the power to develop the right equation in a dark place to bring in the light of wisdom, and project it to others in a ways that can turn them down if they fill turned up.

It is the yen and yang in you that brings together the spiritual light out of a kind of darkness that is naked to the human eye. That makes a life force that automatically protects life substance out of the element of love. The stronger the love of the Lord that you have in you, the stronger the spiritual skills you deliver to his people.

What can I say? It is somewhat like climbing out of a tunnel in the middle of it using the Son of God that the Lord supplies to bring you to the light of a truth you need. It is also like having a group of angels doing the thinking for you and at the same time, using you to act out the actions and reactions you need to in order to make a safe haven at a time there may be a kind of conflict that needs intervention to create resolve, in spite of the darkness that would like to present itself.

To connect with the spiritual skills principals may be the best chance that all people have to outgrow their "isms" in life. What are they? Love thy neighbor as yourself and as you know the Lord loves you.

There is a fact that all peoples of wealth and means are not a towerist in the land they live in but for those who are, they do find themselves stuck in a self-containing spiritual war of their own that by means of understanding this process they can be freed of.

The process of the disconnection of this does not have to have any kind of backlash or repercussion from being in a position that one was not able to dismantle their mindset and spirit from. In Jesus name Amen

One of the Worse; if Not the Worse!

What does the understanding of how to stay out of a battle do for anyone? It helps to not escalate the warfare. The abilities that come with spiritual skills can give this to people.

What can it do to help lots of people who don't know how to stop themselves from harming a loved one after the end of a relationship? They can keep them from putting on blinders and thinking that if they can't have them, in this physical world, they can have them in the next world or spiritual world because they don't have them there.

It is a trick of Satan. The fact of the physical loss of together can run amok to a place that the person at loss goes into a spiritual warfare with themselves and Satan keeps stepping in to push them over the edge in their mental state. They feel all they can do about the loneliness and pain, is harm the one they love and Satan wins. He doesn't win with both parties just the one who commits the sin.

This I get more in-depth about in other books, *Time to Stop the Abuse* and *Time to Stop Living on the Edge*. I am not trying to promote other books I have written but it is what it is.

Let go and let God! Get your covering before it is too late!

The crazy part of the existence of Satan is for anyone that lays hands on God's anointed or chosen people in a way they are not supposed to, he reserves a special spot in hell for you for people who create more torment than the average person can get. Is that a reward that anyone needs or wants to get rushed into?

Take Notice

Take notice that we can place other ducks in a row to take out of our way in order for us to succeed in staying out of the way of any kind of spiritual wars in our mind that we are not in accordance with the Lord's will supposed to be in.

Where was the first spiritual war fought? It was fought in heaven and those who were on the side of Satan were a bit of a handful. That is why only people with a supernatural blessing are able to defend the darkness of Satan's spiritual world off because it takes more than human strength.

A Name of the People Need Not be Mentioned

To create less harm to ourselves and future generations, you may need to rethink your faith and belief. To do harm by mass killings by individuals with dictatorship towerism isn't fair to put one's self and others in that dilemma. We need to break the spiritual ceiling of this inner personal "ism" of warfare of some religious practices and beliefs that go back thousands of years to be able to enter Heaven. Certain people

46

try to make amends at the time of Passover even more so for being in towers while ignoring the sins of their ancestors in the denial of who Jesus is. It won't work!!

What can be done from this way of thinking to help stop the wrong ways and make things right.

We are now on the verge of many new discoveries in our life and time. The one most important discovery we have yet to begin to take on, may be the relationship with our spirituality. That is why we need to head off and end certain problems before they take root and begin to cause disasters are our nation does not need to be a part of. This new level of existence can be developed without added more resistance that comes by way of spiritual warfare.

Who Am I, I Feel

I have the youngest old soul in the world at times. What do I have that helps in and with my life endeavors? I have the spirit of a man over 2,000 years old but it is a spirit of youthfulness.

To the People

This book is not authorized by mankind but authorized by the Lord as a part of his promise that he would be with us to take us through the storms and calm the water. This is truly a part of the intangible presence of an angelic force that the Lord makes available for us as humans. He wants us to make this as it is a part of him and he can be, if we let him, our greatest, brother, father and keeper.

The only way to get to this level of spiritual skills at its fullness is to have a heart of a child of God. It requires nothing greater of you to get started in the spirit of practicing the new skill level of life. The dream land that is made from love land is in your reach.

Now If He Was Chosen By the Lord

May peace and blessings fall upon you from this information like the healing balm of Gilead. Now what could I say about the power of love to stop disasters? As an example, if it was not for Martin Luther King who preached peace, there may have been a kind of spiritual warfare that broke out during the injustices that took place during the time of his ministry? Now this is just a thought to share.

Does the Lord use you and keep what you are doing a secret from you because it might not get done for one reason or another if you knew. It may or may not have been revealed to him that he had more of a mission on earth than he knew about that can stop a war and if he would have not preached peace and he preached hate, it could have started a spiritual war that could have resulted in an untold level of harm that could have bloodied up the country.

Now if a King Couldn't See all, A Towerist Can't See All Also

To prevent it in his heart but not knowing, what could Satan be doing to try to reflect his power on one man to do the same in a way that is the opposite, to cause harm? Now if the other people who can't see what he is doing, and maybe he can't see either they need to be told. Is this what they need to hear?

Is there a man who doesn't know he is being led to have others help to create an outward war level of spiritual warfare that will fall back on them and others? If it is taking place in our country on a small level once they get in the White House and it affects other nations of people, what do you think will happen? Forget about it, you know what will happen, the war of what could be of all time could take place that was put together by Satan using one man.

Now, how can we prevent this? Stop the duck! Don't vote for him for the sake of mankind. That's all folks!

I sometimes like to think of myself as a restorer of things. I would like to restore this one fact that Satan holds dearly as does the Lord. He is also not a respecter of persons. So whatever you think you do in life if the Lord can love you as he loves to, it will be. But if Satan can make you think you can love you for whatever he can make you think you will or need to be he will love you in hate but you can't know it or see it. This blinds, cripples and can make people crazy.

Therefore, let the Lord order your steps because Satan will trick you into believing it is the right step you are taking and it is not.

Knowing all of the things that have been revealed to you can lead you to one conclusion: you now have been presented with the fact that the armor you need to shield yourself and the people from is a measure that cannot be totally explained in a lifetime, but lived through within a certain period of time. Now you know the armor that the Lord has provided has no measurement of length of width or time.

Who is it?

Who needs to take the invisible chip off of their shoulder that they carry around that puts them in the dilemma of self-incrimination of their personal spiritual warfare that affects them to a degree that it adds illness to their lives such as depression, anxiety, deflation of their moral character, insecurity of their ability to accomplish their goals? This list can go on but it can be eliminated with understanding a redevelopment of structuring a spiritual lifestyle that you can acquire with skills of a presence that is holier than yourself.

God's therapy has been applied to the open-minded and the pure in heart.

The equation of facts has been presented. There is no other logical explanation for the illogical way that people who consider themselves to be human and at the same time act like heathens and blood thirsty savages who are performing mass murders on innocent people can't be presented in any other way than they have a spiritual sickness that has them with a spiritual warring factor that comes from the influence of a dictatorship or act of terrorism toward a massive number of people.

This has been displayed throughout history especially in what could be considered undeveloped or underdeveloped parts of the world where people are oppressed and groups of people practice inhumane rituals of darkness and taboo acts of violence toward others. At some point they got caught up in spiritual warfare of a self-incriminating kind.

They lost control of their self-image and self-worth as a human and adopted beastly characteristics with no value for life, whether it is man, woman, child or animal. The inspiration of this could only come from one place, Satan. He used, and still uses, his satanic powers to make people use his tools of darkness to steal, kill and/or destroy the welfare of humankind.

In saying all of this, I am saying that this can be stopped with an understanding that freedom comes from God through faith with the use of wisdom and belief in someone greater than self. We all can have the blessing of the power to not be led by another human or blinding force of darkness on earth, that only creates destruction toward another life.

The new beginning has come to pass. Now it is up to you to know this in your heart and soul, thanks to the Lord.

Now what comes to mind is that we as a people should be on one accord, even if we duck the duck. We should be sure that all of the newly elected presidents from here on should never be put into office if they have towerism; flat out!

So now how about this for a miracle to have a one size fits all when it comes down to a suit of the Lord's armor he puts in or allows you to get in? Now, how about that and at the same time have a forecast of the weather to win not only the race to increase humanity but to increase the volume of Christ-like people on earth.

Know there are too many wins in a column to keep up with the count. Therefore, in other words the word of the Lord, carries the will power to not only do his will, but to see the will he has for the future of life ever after.

What does this statement mean? "these are the results of the big-eyed ones". If you ever saw a child raised with more than enough of their share and they came into a gathering but had no idea of what the process of limitation is all about, they are truly capable of doing one thing: over-indulging themselves until they waste what could be used by someone else where it could be needed. Does that apply to adults also who over-indulge with finance that could be placed somewhere else where it is needed.

In making this statement, all I am interested in is finding a way to help individuals limit their own intake so that it won't create over-take that takes from someone else in need. The process comes down to one thing, how to live with less and gain more. If you have ideas of how we can accomplish this, please share them so that the world can benefit from it.

To the Feast

It is nice for me to present myself as a centerpiece of peace that makes the meal more enjoyable for everyone!

Thank you for all the help you can supply to help increase the numbers to stand for the increasing of human life.

Who am I again? I am one man who was chosen out of many who have the same mindset as so many others who happen to love the fact in my heart that the pen is mightier than war at times in life when it is needed.

Could this information be just what is needed to help prepare some people to go to heaven? Is it what is needed to help save a multitude of people and a part of the destruction of mother earth, in order to keep father time running smoothly? I hope so.

Now, how far are we away from heaven? I think we are no farther away than our heart. It is only just a matter of time to get there. Now, peace be within you and with you.

Now it is time to get off of the edge in the warring way of life that can get people in trouble for an eternity.

Stop spiritual warfare before it
destroys a part of the USA

Philippians 4:17
Not that I seek the gift, but I seek the fruit that
abounds to your account

Acts 20:24
But none of these things move me; nor do I count my life dear to myself, so that I may finish my race with joy, and the ministry which I received from the Lord Jesus, to testify to the gospel of the grace of God.

www.ingramcontent.com/pod-product-compliance
Lightning Source LLC
Chambersburg PA
CBHW071132280526
45787CB00003B/1258